FINDING GOD'S WILL FOR YOUR LIFE

By

Pastor David Newell

In my plus fifty years of serving the Lord, perhaps the most important question I have heard is "what does God want me to do with my life?"

Back in 1965, this was my question. I had had a "Damascus Road" experience with Jesus Christ in 1962. From that moment, I knew the reality and the love that God had for me. But, as far as finding my life's direction, I was perplexed.

I decided to talk with my Dad about it. My father was extremely honest but had real wisdom. I told him I had enjoyed working in the stock market with him, but the thought of working as a stockbroker did not excite me.

My Dad then asked me one question: "Have you asked the Lord what you are to do with your life?" I answered him that I had not. (Truthfully I was apprehensive as to what the Lord might ask me to do, that I did not want to do. In retrospect, when we surrender to the will of God, He gives us the desire He wants us to pursue (Psa.37:4-5).

My Dad said, "all I can say is if you continue to ask Him, He will answer you." I asked him, "but how will I know it?" Dad said simply, "you will know". I took his advice and after about three months of seeking the Lord morning and evening, something changed. Every morning when I got up, the first thing I thought about was ministry and the last thing on my mind when I went to sleep was full time ministry. God was answering me by changing my heart. He took away my apprehensions and put an urgency in my soul.

As you read this booklet, I will give you keys to discovering God's unfolding will for your life. I trust these keys will help you find and embrace God's will for you.'

KEY NUMBER ONE

Know that the Lord has a special plan for you (Jeremiah 29:11; Eph.1:11-13). However, He reveals that plan in steps or stages. The first thing is to make finding that plan the first order of business (Matt.6:33). I have to say that in 1962, when I called on the Lord, repenting of my sins, He saved me and filled me with His love, but after some time, I sensed something was missing. I had no sense of being fulfilled.

KEY NUMBER TWO

We need to pursue the will of God with all our heart. "And you shall seek Me, and find Me, when you search for Me with all your heart" (Jer.29:13). I personally believe the Lord wants to see how serious we are in finding His will. Once I said "yes" to the Lord concerning ministry, the Lord gave me clear direction: "Go to Princeton Theological Seminary and prepare yourself".

KEY NUMBER THREE

When it seems impossible to implement the open door, ask God for wisdom (James 1:5).

When the Lord told me to apply to Princeton, my question to Him was, "my grades in College were only C+/B-, they won't let me in." The Holy Spirit answered, "write a letter to Dr.Ray Lindquist". Dr.Raymond Lindquist was my first pastor. He had rescued my Dad when he was struggling with alcoholism. We were members in his his church in Orange, New Jersey. In 1953 after serving 20 years there, he accepted a call to the Hollywood Presbyterian church in Los Angeles. Ray was a wonderful mentor both to my parents and to me as well.

He quickly responded in a letter. He said as a trustee at the Seminary, he would make sure I was accepted. Soon afterwards, I went for an interview with the Dean of admissions and was accepted with reservations. However now I had clear direction and was committed to give my studies top priority.

KEY NUMBER FOUR

When the Lord opens a door, <u>don't</u> <u>delay</u>, go through it. In 1966, after my first semester at Seminary, my friend Dennis Young and I wanted to take a trip across the country, stopping in Yellowstone and Glacier Park for fishing and sightseeing. However, I sensed the Lord may have another plan. I prayed an insincere prayer: "Lord I will serve wherever you desire, even if it means missing the trip". I even prayed it twice! Within 48 hours, I received a call from a church that were taking their youth group to Florida. Even though I had not volunteered for anything, they found my name (I wonder how that happened,lol?).

I stammered and knew I had been found out! I lied saying, "I'll have to pray about it". In reality, I had no intention of doing God's will for me that summer. The Lord revealed what was in my heart.

My friend and I went on the trip but the first week I was miserable. Finally, I repented and told the Lord, "I will not do this again. If I am still in Your good graces, please open a door for ministry in the fall.I WILL go through that door." At the end of the first week, I called home and my mother told me she had received a call from Jerry Mills, the pastor of

St.Cloud Presbyterian church in West Orange. Pastor Jerry wanted to know if I would be available to serve as the youth pastor in the fall? I told her, "tell him YES!"

KEY NUMBER FIVE

See and understand the reason for the "season" you are in at the time. "To everything there is a season, and a time to every purpose under the heaven" (Eccl.3:1).

In 1967, the Lord opened a door for ministry that summer. The location was Davenport, New York, not far from Oneonta and Cooperstown. Besides preaching in three churches, I had to visit everyone in those churches and lead in the vacation Bible class in the Davenport Presbyterian church.

After being there one month, I began to wonder what specific purpose did the Lord have for me that summer? I made that my prayer going into the second month. Then a series of events happened that answered my question.

First of all, one of the members of the Davenport church, Sonny MacCracken, was rushed to the hospital after suffering a heart attack. I received a call and immediately made my way to the hospital. Although we did not know it at the time, he died in the emergency room. Right after arriving at the hospital, I gathered the family together and we held hands and prayed for the Lord to touch Sonny and heal him. The Lord answered our prayers and he was restored.

After that incident, a special bond was forged between myself and the MacCracken family. Soon afterwards, I sensed the Lord desired me to host a special Billy Graham movie called "Sign of the Boomerang". It was set in Australia and the storyline centered around a family who would wind up in Billy's crusade. There was a strong repentance theme and I had used it in the past with success.

I received permission from the principal of the high school in Davenport to use the gymnasium for showing the movie. I sent letters out to a number of area churches inviting them and to bring the lost. It would be a way to reach the lost and add them to their churches. We trained altar workers and even had a young lady ready to play the Crusade theme song "Just As I am".

On Friday night of the event, the gym was packed and everyone was excited. We ran the movie and when I gave the altar call, no one moved. After a little while I thanked everyone for coming and dismissed them. I was very disappointed. The devil beat me up pretty well, letting me know how feeble my efforts were. I went back to the place where I was staying and had a cup of coffee with the family. They were very supportive and were touched by the movie. At that time of my life I did not know the scripture where God promises His word will not return to Him void (Isa.55:11).

All of a sudden the phone rang. It was Frank MacCracken, Sonny's brother calling. Frank was a dairy farmer and an elder at the Davenport church. He said, "Dave, I told Peg my wife, I wanted someone to respond to that powerful message in the movie, and she said to me' 'Frank wouldn't it be something if that person was you'"! Then Frank began to tell me that he had never really taken the message of the Gospel of Jesus Christ seriously but he was ready for that to change. From that moment on that family would never be the same.

Fast forwarding, in 1982 Frank and Peg planted a church in Maryland, New York and we formally ordained them the next year. Frank pastored for the next 10 years, giving the church over to his son Frank Jr. who is currently the senior pastor there. The Lord will show you the purpose for the season you are in.

KEY NUMBER 6

The Lord will often speak on both ends in making sure you receive the direction you need. In the spring of 1968, I was asking the Lord what foundation stone He wanted to set in place in my life? I had been water baptized and baptized in the Holy Spirit. I learned that within a few weeks there would be a prophetic presbytery formed to minister prophetic direction for God's people. Leading up to these meetings, I had been in a time of fasting and prayer, as I wanted the Holy Spirit to wash me afresh and set me apart. I even wrote out a "spiritual inventory", of areas of my life I needed to experience freedom.

That very afternoon in the meeting at Philadelphia Gospel Temple in east Philly, I was called out and knelt before several prophets who did not know me at all. One prophet, Charles Green, a pastor from New Orleans, prophesied that God was stripping me of every thing I would count on in the natural. He went on to say if I would allow the Lord to accomplish His work, He would send me across the nation with signs following. He would eventually bring me to a city where I would plant a New Covenant church. Right after the service I ran to talk with Pastor Green as he was leaving for the airport. I told him what would he say if I told him the Lord wanted me to join him for the summer to be mentored until I had to return to Princeton. As he was getting into the car, he said that the Lord had spoken the same thing to him and that he would call me in my dorm room the following Sunday afternoon.

KEY NUMBER SEVEN

When you receive direction from the Lord, don't let anyone talk you out of it. As my time at the Seminary was ending, I began to inquire of the Lord if I should stay in the Presbyterian church. I had been disturbed by the change in the Westminster Confession which validated the inerrancy of God's Word. The new Confession was called the Confession of 1967, which was much more vague in its declaration of the authority of God's Word.

In addition, I had issues with infant baptism. In addition, I was newly baptized in the Holy Spirit with speaking in tongues and wondered how wise it would be to stay in that denomination. Thinking things through prayerfully, I came to the conclusion that if I would stay there, one of two things would happen: I would either split a church down the middle or compromise and hide my light under a bushel. Neither alternative seemed right. The peace of God settled on me that I should come out of the denomination.

Soon after that I set up a meeting with one of the pastor's at the Gospel Temple and we went out for dessert after an evening service. I told him what the Lord had spoken to me and I thought he would confirm it, as he was in a non-denominational church. Instead, he did everything possible to talk me out of my decision. Exasperated, I politely but firmly told him I was definite in my decision to leave but thanked him for his time. Then something strange happened.He began to laugh. I asked him what was funny? He said "I had to test you. If I could talk you out of your decision, then I believed you made the decision on your own, but if I couldn't then I believed you did hear from God.

I told him where did that wisdom come from? He said Elijah tried to talk Elisha out of following him three times but Elisha had heard from God he was to be Elijah's replacement (2 Kings 2:1-8).

KEY NUMBER 8

You can ask the Lord for confirmation concerning His purpose. "...in the mouth of two or three witnesses shall every word be established" (2 Cor.13:1).

In 1969, the Lord had opened a door for me to go to Annapolis, Maryland to help my friend, Charlie Beck establish a church in the Davidsonville area. I had just graduated from Seminary and needed practical experience teaching the Word.

In those days we were involved in the "home church" movement. I came totally by faith, and the Lord supplied all my needs.

Charlie and I were teaching four nights in different homes and as a result my days were free. Most days I was in the Word about six hours a day. Interestingly, a prophecy had come one month before I arrived saying the Lord was raising up a "Joshua-Caleb" ministry to bring the church into "the land" (of God's Promises).

The day I arrived, the prophetic word came confirming I was the Caleb part and Charlie the

Joshua, as founding pastor six months prior. Sundays we would each minister as well.

After six months, the Holy Spirit spoke to me as I sat under a tree following a workout near the Sevrin River. The Lord said "as Caleb went into Hebron and possessed his possessions, so I am sending you to your Hebron. Their you will begin the next phase of your ministry". I immediately knew my "Hebron" was to return to New Orleans, where I had served with Pastor Charles Green as an intern the previous summer. I thanked the Lord and trusted He would speak on the other end to Pastor Green.

God gave me that word on a Saturday in July. The next day I arrived in church without letting people know what God had said. Right after worship, one of the elders came up to me and said publically, "Caleb, hear the word of the Lord. Even as Caleb went into Hebron and possessed his possessions, so shall you now arise and go to your Hebron." It was almost word for word what the Holy Spirit said to me the day before! As it worked out, I called Pastor Green the next day and reported to him what the Lord had said. He was excited and said to come in two weeks. He had work for me to do and could pay me $50 a week. God knows how to confirm His direction in our lives as we take the first step.

KEY NUMBER NINE

Be open to "secondary direction". You know the specific purpose God has for you. However, in conjunction with that, a secondary or smaller door opens that will not take away from your main purpose. Go through it.

After leaving Annapolis, I went to New Orleans, where I was ordained at Word of Faith Temple (what it was called in the summer of 1969). I had regular ministerial duties but one afternoon something interesting happened.

After lunch and an early afternoon run, I made my way to the "upper room" where we went to pray before service. There was one lady in that room, Juanita Ebrenz. I went to the other side of the room to pray. When I was finished, I got up and walked over to Mrs. Ebrenz. I put my hand on her shoulder and said, "Lord, give my sister grace for the ministry she has just started". I knew nothing about what she was doing at the time, only that the Lord had spoken to me.

Immediately, she reached up and grabbed my arm, pulling me down to eye level with her. She said, "You are right, I have just started a ministry in the ninth ward on St.Maurice Street. I am teaching a number of children. But there are about 18 African American teens who need to teacher. I asked the Lord if that teacher was you, for you to come over here and speak the words you spoke over me just now".

The Lord had me. I knew there was no way I could back out. I had not asked for this, but as she spoke those words, I sensed the Lord saying "this is of Me".

I have to admit, I was in fear and trembling, as I had no idea what to expect or if I would be received at all. I asked the Lord what I should teach? He said My Lordship , the Power of My Blood and Repentance. "How long do I teach on this Lord?" His answer: "Until they repent, are saved and make Me their Lord!".

Miraculously, after several months, many were saved and two teens (had been dating) were not only saved but committed to preach the Gospel. The outcome : a church was eventually established and is functioning to this day.

KEY NUMBER TEN

Always follow the peace. "And let the peace of God rule in your hearts" (Col.3:15). The J.B.Phillips translation says, "let the peace of God umpire in your hearts". The umpire always has the last say in a baseball game.

A lot was going on with me in the fall of 1969. In September I got engaged. I got engaged to a girl in a Spirit filled church in Baton Rouge and would drive over on Friday in the late afternoon and return to New Orleans late in the evening.

As our relationship ensued, I found myself losing my peace about the upcoming wedding. Then one Saturday morning I received a phone call from Charles and Barbara Green, my pastors. They wanted to see me right away. Almost as soon as I entered their house, they began to tearfully beseech me to reconsider the marriage. They did not have any peace about it either.

I shared with them how God had been dealing with me that I should break off the engagement. My fiance was a fine girl but just not who the Lord had for me.

Once we met and broke off the engagement, peace returned to me and even my ex-fiance felt a peace as well.

Several months later, while at a College and Career party at the Green's, Barbara mentioned to me she knew a girl who would be a "tremendous pastor's wife". Leaning down I said "who is that?" She said Ina Johnson. I knew Ina from the youth group. She played piano and was a student at Loyola University, pursuing a career as a dental hygienist. To make a long story short, we began dating in February of 1970 and were married on November 7, 1970. Just before we were married, we went to the church on a Friday evening after seeing the movie "Camelot". We both felt drawn to commit our marriage to the Lord. No one was at the church. We went into the prayer room and began to seek the Lord for our soon coming marriage.

Suddenly, the Glory Cloud of the Lord enveloped us. We could literally see it. We were caught up in His Presence and lost track of time. The Lord put His Amen on our marriage for which we are eternally grateful. Needless to say, we both followed God's peace.

KEY NUMBER 11

Are there such things as "contradictions" in God's leadership? Listen to Hebrews 12:3: "For consider Him that endured such a contradiction of sinners against Himself, lest you be wearied and faint in your minds".

In September of 1992, the Holy Spirit spoke to me that within 9 months Ina and I would be moving and pastoring a church. Exactly 9 months later, we received an invitation to pastor a church in Shreveport, Louisiana. We were released and sent forth with the blessings of Pastor Green and the congregation we helped pastor for 25 years. It was a bittersweet time but we knew it was the will of God. Just before leaving, Pastor Green met with me and said he had been praying and believed we would not be there a long time but the Lord would lead us to a church plant that we would pastor for a long time.

As it turned out, we were there from October 1993 until May of 1996. It was a time of God's dealings with us as a family. Every facet of our lives were tested. Finally, the Lord told us to turn the church over to the elders and leave. He told us that He was sending me across the nation (beginning the second phase of the prophetic word He had given me in

1968). We had no money and not much in the way of prospects.I will tell you how all that changed with my next "Key". We left at a real low time emotionally. I inquired of the Lord what were His reasons for bringing us to that area? What did He want to accomplish in us? He spoke very clearly from Hosea 2:14-16:

"Therefore, behold, I will allure her, and bring her into the wilderness (that was us) and speak comfortably unto her. And I will give her her vineyards from thence(where we would minister) and the Valley of Achor (Weeping) for a door of hope: and she shall sing there as in the days of her youth, and as in the day when she came up out of the land of Egypt. And it shall be at that day, saith the Lord, that you shall call me Husband and you shall no longer call me Master."

Here is what the Lord told me. " You and Ina have always been strong soldiers for Me. However, I allowed you to go through some suffering to bring you back to knowing Me as your Husband, One who loves you both greatly."

It is easy to get off track and major in the minors. The suffering we go through can be used by the

Lord to bring us back to our first love and receiving His love that heals all wounds.

As we moved on from there, over the next year as I traveled, I would spend much time soaking in God's Presence and love.

KEY NUMBER 12

Realize prophetic fulfillment can take time. The first prophetic word I received was in 1968. I was called out of the congregation and was told by the prophets the Lord would strip me of everything I would trust in, and if I let the Lord do His bidding, there would come a time He would send me across the nation as an evangelist with signs following. Also, after that time, the Lord would lead me to plant a New Testament church in a city He had selected.

From the time I received that word until the time God fulfilled His word spanned 29 years. "Though the vision tarry, wait for it, it shall surely speak.." (Habb.2:1-2).

KEY NUMBER 13

Realize prophetic fulfillment can take a short time. In October of 1996, I was in Charlotte, North Carolina participating in a prophetic conference. After a class I taught, I went into another classroom where a prophet named Ed Traut was teaching and ministering. I sat in the back of the classroom and waited until he was finished and it was time for lunch.

I was walking out the door when Pastor Ed asked if we could walk together to the dining room. As we walked, he asked me what the Lord was saying to me for the coming year (1997)? I told him the Lord had spoken to Ina and I to plant a church. Ed said he bore witness to that and then asked if he could give me the word of the Lord.

He said "You are a foundation layer. The city you came from rejected your ministry but you kept your spirit right. God is giving you a sign: just before you plant your church, God will vindicate you from the city that rejected you."

I was stunned but encouraged. I had no clue as to how the Lord would fulfill that word, but I trusted Him to bring it to pass.

In January of 1997, while I was preaching in Michigan, Ina received a call from Guidepost Magazine. The person on the other end wanted me to call them as soon as possible. As I returned the call, I found out an article had been submitted by David Westerfield who was a feature writer from the Shreveport Times and a member of our church in that city. David had suffered from a virus in the brain that disabled him to the point he could not sit up without getting physically ill. This malady went on for months. Much prayer from the church had gone up for David. Then one day, just before I left Shreveport, I paid one last visit to David in The hospital. As the visit went on, the Presence of the Lord moved into the room. He and his wife and I began to laugh with God's joy (and there was nothing funny). We all sensed the Lord was doing something special for David.

It was not until later, speaking with the representative from Guidepost, that I found out David had received a miracle. He had submitted an article to Guidepost giving God the glory and talking about my visit. The person on the phone let me know they were going to publish his testimony as long as I confirmed the reality of the event. Of course I did and the article appeared in the May

1997 issue of Guidepost, one month before we established River of Life Church in Raleigh, North Carolina. God is so good!

KEY NUMBER 13

I want to give you a back story to the last key. It involves forgiveness. In May of 1996 the Lord indicated He wanted Ina and I to resign and turn the church over to our elders. I did and began to make plans to "go on the road". But before the Lord opened the next door for us, I must mention some very important things.

First of all, some people from the church approached us to split off from the church and form a new church. But Ina had received a word from the Lord to "not split the baby". This was drawn from the story in 2 Kings chapter 3 where Solomon is confronted by two women claiming to be the mother of one of two children who survived one mother's accidentally smothering her baby in the night. The mother who did this said "why not divide the child by the sword"? The real mother cried "No!" "Give her to the lady who had lost her child". Solomon instantly knew who the real mother was, not dividing the baby but giving her to the real mother.

Ina shared her word with me and I was in total agreement. We were to leave with peace in our hearts. But before we actually resigned, we were in the midst of some extreme pressure to the point that Ina said to me she felt the best thing to do was for her to take two of our sons and head west. She said to me I could take the other. She was not mad at me but did not know what to do with the pressure and perhaps I could join her out west later. Needless to say I was heart broken. We actually both wept and held each other.

Ina said she would meet me later in the afternoon but had to go on an errand. She had not gone more than several miles when the Lord spoke to her, telling her we had chosen well not to split "the baby" (the church). He said that He would lead us and to set a time when we would hand in our resignation. She called me and we were both laughing and crying at the same time.

Soon after we resigned, the Holy Spirit spoke to me to go to a man's office in Shreveport and bless him and his business. This man was an elder at the church and was one who was glad to see me go. I was not thrilled to hear this but obeyed. We did not speak much, but I told him I had come to bless his business if he was willing. He accepted and we prayed and I blessed him and the business.

Several weeks went by and I received a very warm letter from him. He related how it looked like he was going to have to declare bankruptcy but after I blessed his business, everything turned around for him. He asked for forgiveness for his actions toward us (which I had already forgave). Right after that, many doors opened for traveling ministry.

In December of 1996, Ina and I were in conducting prophetic ministry in Carthage, Missouri at Pastor J.P. Wilson's church. After the last service, one of his elder's approached Ina and I with a word from the Lord. He said that there was one person we needed to forgive to his face. (He knew nothing about our situation). He went on to say we may have already forgiven him in our hearts (we had) but we needed to do this for his sake. I put this brother on the spot, asking if he had a vision of what this man looked like. He did and described him to a "t".

When we returned to Shreveport (I traveled for one year between May 1996 and May of 1997), we drove over to this other elder's house. It was Christmas Eve. They were both surprised to see us but his wife asked us to come in. Ina and I let them know we were there to put everything under the Blood of Christ. We asked them to forgive us for anyway we may have hurt them. His wife responded saying, "We are the ones that need to ask your forgiveness". We forgave, held hands and prayed. Soon afterwards God opened a large door for us to come to Raleigh to plant River of Life church.

KEY NUMBER 14

The Lord is concerned about everything relating to His children and making sure we received His direction concerning the name of the church we were going to plant. We love how His hand guides us, even mixing His sense of humor into His direction.

During the fall of 1996, Ina and I had been invited to Tulsa to Phil Stern's church to attend a prophetic presbytery. Phil's Dad, Paul was there as part of the Presbytery. (Paul had been a powerful missionary in Kenya and later founded a church in Illinois).

We were called to receive a prophetic word very soon after the conference began. One of the visiting prophet's, Moses Veigh (who knew nothing about us) spoke a word that he saw a mighty river of life flowing from Ina and I, watering many old thirsty camels. We laughed but the thought "River of Life" stuck and we sensed the Lord wanted us to call the church River of Life.

KEY NUMBER 15

Jesus, our Shepherd, knows who we need to be connected to in order to bring His will to pass. God will connect you to the right people in order to fulfill His will in your life. It will be an adventure and it will be wonderful.

In February of 1997, I returned after being on the the road for awhile. Ina and Matthew (then a senior in high school) had found a great church in Shreveport. Pastor Artis Cash was the founder and a very prophetic man. That week, Pastor Cash had invited me to go on his TV program and talk about racial reconciliation.

While waiting to go on the set, He asked me what the Lord was telling me for this new year. I told him God had spoken to us to plant a church, but did not tell him where. Pastor Cash asked if he could give me a word. I said absolutely!

He then related it was in the Raleigh-Durham area of North Carolina. That we should move on it. He even laid out strategies which would employ. He even said he would pay for one month of radio time to help get the work going. We accepted.

The next day, we received a phone call from Pastor Charles Green. We had not spoken with him for several years. He asked me "what is the Lord telling you for this new year?" I told him Ina and I were being led to do a church plant but did not mention the location. He asked if he could give us a word? We agreed. He said "it is in the Raleigh-Durham area of North Carolina and we were to move on it!

When it is time for God to move, He will make His purpose very clear!

KEY NUMBER 16

At times, we will be tested to see if we will actually push through and do the will of God, especially when there are seeming roadblocks.

Once we knew the Lord was wanting to us to move, we put our house up for sale. We had been buying the house from a retired business man in the neighborhood. We mentioned to Pastor Cash did he know anyone who might want to buy the house? He did. He said there was a couple in his church who were looking for a house. Both had good jobs and we showed them the house. They were excited. Pastor Cash told me privately if they could not make the payments, the church would buy the house and use it to house visiting ministry. He went on to say they would co-sign if necessary.

We spoke to the owner and he was excited. The agreement was that the buyers would give me back the downpayment and assume the loan we had with this gentleman. Just before leaving this man's house, I told him I did not want him stunned at the closing. We told him the couple buying the house were African Americans. The color drained from his face and he hung his head. He said "I can't do this, I am afraid of my neighbors. I guess I am not a very good Christian?" I said to him, "you said it out of your own mouth."

As it turned out we gave the house back to him, he said we owed him nothing (we settled this in a lawyer's office). We forsook our down payment as well because the Lord wanted us to make the move quickly.

We made two trips to North Carolina (only knew one couple in Durham) before we moved. On the second trip, we asked David and Lynn Johnson to join us and give us prayer covering. The Johnson's had become close to us during our years in New Orleans. Just before leaving on that Monday morning, we had breakfast together at the hotel where they were staying. At the end of the meal, we prayed together and they handed us an envelope with a check for $9000 to help us get what we would need for a church start up (we would meet in hotels for the first few years but needed microphones and sound equipment).

Three years later, we moved into a 3800 square foot home in Cary, North Carolina. Ina found the house and we got it at a greatly reduced price. At that time all three sons and Ina's mother were living with us, helping get the church going. We needed the room. The Lord will always recompense us for whatever we do or spend for His Kingdom!

Ina and I trust this little booklet has been a help to you in learning to be led by the Holy Spirit. Remember, God wants a relationship with you every day. He is concerned with the large and the small things in your life.

Manifesting the Father's love,

Standing in the

Finished work of Jesus,

Celebrating the

Presence

of the Holy Spirit!

www.riverofliferaleigh.com

God loves it when His children pray and He wants our prayers to be a constant source of encouragement and hope. **We invite you to fill out the prayer request form on our website, and our church family will pray for you.** Simply fill out the form and submit. The word of God and prayers work yesterday, today, and tomorrow! Amazing things happen when God's people pray.

"....for my house will be called a house of prayer for all peoples." **Isaiah 56:7**

GOD'S DREAM FOR RIVER OF LIFE CHURCH

1 Cor.15:10

The Gospel of Grace is the answer to the "disinformation" the enemy has used to blind and bind the Church for decades. (Def. :intentionally false and inaccurate information; to convince of untruth). Ex- Normandy landing.

The Lord has been seeding us with Truth to combat this disinformation. This is the CHANGE that is occurring. We have been in a time of Transformation and that period of time is Finishing. God's Church is transitioning from Legalism to Grace. He is Revealing the full revelation of Grace which brings change. The next stage is to RUN with the message.

NOTES

Made in the USA
Columbia, SC
25 May 2023